POLAND
WORLD ADVENTURES
BY GEMMA McMULLEN

BookLife

©2016
Book Life
King's Lynn
Norfolk PE30 4LS

ISBN: 978-1-910512-63-0

Written by:
Gemma McMullen
Edited by:
Harriet Brundle
Designed by:
Drue Rintoul

A catalogue record for this book
is available from the British Library.

POLAND
WORLD ADVENTURES

CONTENTS

Page 4   Where is Poland?

Page 6   Weather and Landscape

Page 8   Clothing

Page 10   Religion

Page 12   Food

Page 14   At School

Page 16   At Home

Page 18   Families

Page 20   Sport

Page 22   Fun Facts

Page 24   Glossary and Index

Words in **bold** can be found in the glossary on page 24.

WHERE IS POLAND?

POLAND

Poland is a large country located in central Europe. The capital city of Poland is called Warsaw. The Polish flag is white and red.

WARSAW

More than 38 million people live in Poland but many Polish people choose to live and work **abroad**.

WEATHER AND LANDSCAPE

Poland has a mostly cold **climate**, although it can get quite hot in the summer. The winters are cold and snowy, especially in the mountains located in the south of the country.

The land in the north of Poland is largely flat. There are some lovely coastal beaches.

CLOTHING

In everyday life, Polish clothes are practical and are worn to suit the weather outside. **Traditional** costumes are sometimes still worn on special occasions.

8

The costumes are different in different areas of the country, but are usually brightly coloured with **embroidery**. Headdresses or hats are worn by men and women.

RELIGION

The religion most followed in Poland is Christianity. Many of the Christians are Roman Catholic.

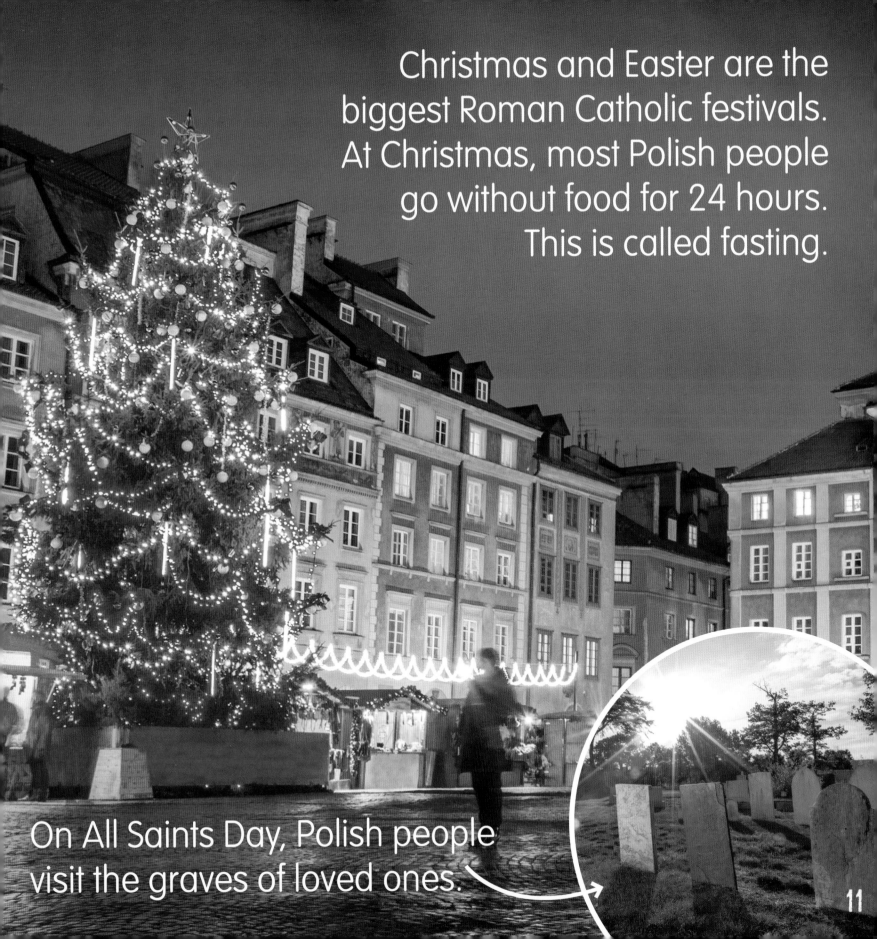

Christmas and Easter are the biggest Roman Catholic festivals. At Christmas, most Polish people go without food for 24 hours. This is called fasting.

On All Saints Day, Polish people visit the graves of loved ones.

FOOD

One of the **national** dishes of Poland is bigos, a meat and cabbage stew. Another popular food is golabki, which is meat wrapped in cabbage leaves and served in sauce.

BIGOS

GOLABKI

Polish people eat four meals a day. They have two breakfasts, one early in the morning and another later on.

AT SCHOOL

Polish children start school at the age of six or seven and leave between the ages of eighteen and twenty. Schools run from September to June.

Lessons at Polish schools include Polish, maths, science, history and geography. Polish children do not wear uniforms to school.

AT HOME

Modern Polish homes are similar to those found in Britain. They are made of brick so that they are strong. Polish homes have central heating and double-glazed windows to keep them warm.

Many Polish homes have gardens, which are great spaces for children to play in.

FAMILIES

Most Polish children live with their parents and **siblings**.

Family is very important in Poland. Polish people value family more than money or their jobs. They keep in touch with family members even when they move away.

Sunday dinner at home is a tradition that Polish families stick to.

SPORT

The most popular sport in Poland is football. Other popular sports include hockey, basketball and motorbike speedway.

The Polish mountains are a good place for hiking, skiing and mountain biking and get a lot of **tourists** every year from all over the world. Cross country skiing and ski jumping are popular on TV.

FUN FACTS

Poland's national symbol is the White Eagle.

The Polish alphabet has 32 letters.

A Ą B C Ć D E Ę
F G H I J K L Ł
M N Ń O Ó P R S
Ś T U W Y Z Ź Ż

Polish athlete Mariusz Pudzianowski won the 'World's Strongest Man' competition five times.

There isn't any tomato sauce on the pizzas in Poland, the sauce is served separately!

GLOSSARY

abroad: in another country

climate: the weather in an area

embroidery: a rasied pattern sewn into fabric

modern: something that has been made using recent ideas

national: common to a nation

siblings: brothers and sisters

tourists: visitors from another country

traditional: ways of behaving that have been done for a long time

INDEX

bigos: 12

Catholic: 10, 11

children: 14, 15, 17, 18

costume: 8, 9

golabki: 12

school: 14, 15

summer: 6

Warsaw: 4, 5

winter: 6